The Ultimate Weekly Planner

for Successful Korean Business People

A c t i v i n o t e s

Activinotes

DAILY JOURNALS, PLANNERS, NOTEBOOKS AND OTHER BLANK BOOKS

Weeekly Planner

○ Monday

○ Tuesday

○ Wednesday

○ Thursday

라이브 생활

○ Friday

○ Saturday

○ Sunday

NOTES

{FILE IT}

MONEY

TAXES

MEDICAL

HOME

AUTO

BUSINESS

{SPENDING CHECKLIST}

ITEM	NEED	WANT

{NOTES}

Weeekly Planner

○ Monday

○ Tuesday

○ Wednesday

○ Thursday

라이브 생활

○ Friday

○ Saturday

○ Sunday

NOTES

{FILE IT}

MONEY

TAXES

MEDICAL

HOME

AUTO

BUSINESS

{SPENDING CHECKLIST}

ITEM	NEED	WANT

{NOTES}

Weeekly Planner

○ Monday

○ Tuesday

○ Wednesday

○ Thursday

라이브 생활

○ Friday

○ Saturday

○ Sunday

NOTES

{FILE IT}

MONEY

TAXES

MEDICAL

HOME

AUTO

BUSINESS

{SPENDING CHECKLIST}

ITEM	NEED	WANT

{NOTES}

_____

_____

_____

_____

_____

_____

_____

_____

_____

Weeekly Planner

○ Monday

○ Tuesday

○ Wednesday

○ Thursday

◯ Friday

◯ Saturday

◯ Sunday

NOTES

{FILE IT}

MONEY

TAXES

MEDICAL

HOME

AUTO

BUSINESS

{SPENDING CHECKLIST}

ITEM	NEED	WANT

{NOTES}

Weeekly Planner

○ Monday

○ Tuesday

○ Wednesday

○ Thursday

라이브 생활

○ Friday

○ Saturday

○ Sunday

NOTES

{FILE IT}

MONEY

TAXES

MEDICAL

HOME

AUTO

BUSINESS

{SPENDING CHECKLIST}

ITEM	NEED	WANT

{NOTES}

Weeekly Planner

◯ Monday

◯ Tuesday

◯ Wednesday

◯ Thursday

◯ Friday

◯ Saturday

◯ Sunday

NOTES

{FILE IT}

MONEY

TAXES

MEDICAL

HOME

AUTO

BUSINESS

{SPENDING CHECKLIST}

ITEM	NEED	WANT

{NOTES}

_____

_____

_____

_____

_____

_____

_____

_____

Weeekly Planner

○ Monday

○ Tuesday

○ Wednesday

○ Thursday

◯ Friday

◯ Saturday

◯ Sunday

NOTES

{FILE IT}

MONEY

TAXES

MEDICAL

HOME

AUTO

BUSINESS

{SPENDING CHECKLIST}

ITEM	NEED	WANT

{NOTES}

_____

_____

_____

_____

_____

_____

_____

_____

_____

Weeekly Planner

○ Monday

○ Tuesday

○ Wednesday

○ Thursday

라이브 생활

○ Friday

○ Saturday

○ Sunday

NOTES

{FILE IT}

MONEY

TAXES

MEDICAL

HOME

AUTO

BUSINESS

{SPENDING CHECKLIST}

ITEM	NEED	WANT

{NOTES}

Weeekly Planner

○ Monday

○ Tuesday

○ Wednesday

○ Thursday

라이브 생활

⭘ Friday

⭘ Saturday

⭘ Sunday

NOTES

{FILE IT}

MONEY

TAXES

MEDICAL

HOME

AUTO

BUSINESS

{SPENDING CHECKLIST}

ITEM	NEED	WANT

{NOTES}

_____
_____
_____
_____
_____
_____
_____
_____
_____

Weeekly Planner

◯ Monday

◯ Tuesday

◯ Wednesday

◯ Thursday

라이브 생활

○ Friday

○ Saturday

○ Sunday

NOTES

{FILE IT}

MONEY

TAXES

MEDICAL

HOME

AUTO

BUSINESS

{SPENDING CHECKLIST}

ITEM	NEED	WANT

{NOTES}

Weeekly Planner

○ Monday

○ Tuesday

○ Wednesday

○ Thursday

라이브 생활

○ Friday

○ Saturday

○ Sunday

NOTES

{FILE IT}

MONEY

TAXES

MEDICAL

HOME

AUTO

BUSINESS

{SPENDING CHECKLIST}

ITEM	NEED	WANT

{NOTES}

Weeekly Planner

⃝ Monday

⃝ Tuesday

⃝ Wednesday

⃝ Thursday

◯ Friday

◯ Saturday

◯ Sunday

NOTES

{FILE IT}

MONEY

TAXES

MEDICAL

HOME

AUTO

BUSINESS

{SPENDING CHECKLIST}

ITEM	NEED	WANT

{NOTES}

Weeekly Planner

○ Monday

○ Tuesday

○ Wednesday

○ Thursday

라이브 생활

⚪ Friday

⚪ Saturday

⚪ Sunday

NOTES

{FILE IT}

MONEY

TAXES

MEDICAL

HOME

AUTO

BUSINESS

{SPENDING CHECKLIST}

ITEM	NEED	WANT

{NOTES}

Weeekly Planner

○ Monday

○ Tuesday

○ Wednesday

○ Thursday

◯ Friday

◯ Saturday

◯ Sunday

NOTES

{FILE IT}

MONEY

TAXES

MEDICAL

HOME

AUTO

BUSINESS

{SPENDING CHECKLIST}

ITEM	NEED	WANT

{NOTES}

_____

_____

_____

_____

_____

_____

_____

_____

_____

Weeekly Planner

○ Monday

○ Tuesday

○ Wednesday

○ Thursday

◯ Friday

◯ Saturday

◯ Sunday

NOTES

{FILE IT}

MONEY

TAXES

MEDICAL

HOME

AUTO

BUSINESS

{SPENDING CHECKLIST}

ITEM	NEED	WANT

{NOTES}

Weeekly Planner

○ Monday

○ Tuesday

○ Wednesday

○ Thursday

○ Friday

○ Saturday

○ Sunday

NOTES

{FILE IT}

MONEY

TAXES

MEDICAL

HOME

AUTO

BUSINESS

{SPENDING CHECKLIST}

ITEM	NEED	WANT

{NOTES}

Weeekly Planner

○ Monday

○ Tuesday

○ Wednesday

○ Thursday

라이브 생활

○ Friday

○ Saturday

○ Sunday

NOTES

{FILE IT}

MONEY

TAXES

MEDICAL

HOME

AUTO

BUSINESS

{SPENDING CHECKLIST}

ITEM	NEED	WANT

{NOTES}

Weeekly Planner

◯ Monday

◯ Tuesday

◯ Wednesday

◯ Thursday

⭕ **Friday**

⭕ **Saturday**

⭕ **Sunday**

NOTES

{FILE IT}

MONEY

TAXES

MEDICAL

HOME

AUTO

BUSINESS

{SPENDING CHECKLIST}

ITEM	NEED	WANT

{NOTES}

_____

_____

_____

_____

_____

_____

_____

_____

_____

_____

Weeekly Planner

○ Monday

○ Tuesday

○ Wednesday

○ Thursday

◯ Friday

◯ Saturday

◯ Sunday

NOTES

{FILE IT}

MONEY

TAXES

MEDICAL

HOME

AUTO

BUSINESS

{SPENDING CHECKLIST}

ITEM	NEED	WANT

{NOTES}

Weeekly Planner

○ Monday

○ Tuesday

○ Wednesday

○ Thursday

라이브 생활

○ Friday

○ Saturday

○ Sunday

NOTES

{FILE IT}

MONEY

TAXES

MEDICAL

HOME

AUTO

BUSINESS

{SPENDING CHECKLIST}

ITEM	NEED	WANT

{NOTES}

Weeekly Planner

○ Monday

○ Tuesday

○ Wednesday

○ Thursday

라이브 생활

○ Friday

○ Saturday

○ Sunday

NOTES

{FILE IT}

MONEY	
TAXES	
MEDICAL	
HOME	
AUTO	
BUSINESS	

{SPENDING CHECKLIST}

ITEM	NEED	WANT

{NOTES}

Weeekly Planner

○ Monday

○ Tuesday

○ Wednesday

○ Thursday

○ Friday

○ Saturday

○ Sunday

NOTES

{FILE IT}

MONEY

TAXES

MEDICAL

HOME

AUTO

BUSINESS

{SPENDING CHECKLIST}

ITEM	NEED	WANT

{NOTES}

Weeekly Planner

○ Monday

○ Tuesday

○ Wednesday

○ Thursday

○ Friday

○ Saturday

○ Sunday

NOTES

{FILE IT}

MONEY

TAXES

MEDICAL

HOME

AUTO

BUSINESS

{SPENDING CHECKLIST}

ITEM	NEED	WANT

{NOTES}

Weeekly Planner

○ Monday

○ Tuesday

○ Wednesday

○ Thursday

○ Friday

○ Saturday

○ Sunday

NOTES

{FILE IT}

MONEY	

TAXES	

MEDICAL	

HOME	

AUTO	

BUSINESS	

{SPENDING CHECKLIST}

ITEM	NEED	WANT

{NOTES}

Weeekly Planner

○ Monday

○ Tuesday

○ Wednesday

○ Thursday

라이브 생활

○ Friday

○ Saturday

○ Sunday

NOTES

{FILE IT}

MONEY

TAXES

MEDICAL

HOME

AUTO

BUSINESS

{SPENDING CHECKLIST}

ITEM	NEED	WANT

{NOTES}

_____

_____

_____

_____

_____

_____

_____

_____

_____

Weeekly Planner

○ Monday

○ Tuesday

○ Wednesday

○ Thursday

◯ Friday

◯ Saturday

◯ Sunday

NOTES

{FILE IT}

MONEY

TAXES

MEDICAL

HOME

AUTO

BUSINESS

www.ingramcontent.com/pod-product-compliance
Lightning Source LLC
Chambersburg PA
CBHW050906100426
42737CB00048B/3194